From the Farm to the Table Olives

by

Kathy Coatney

Copyright @ 2012, 2014 by Kathy Coatney

www.kathycoatney.com

From the Farm to the Table Series
From the Farm to the Table: Olives
Book 3

All rights reserved

No part of this publication can be reproduced or transmitted in any form or by any means, electronic or mechanical, without permission in writing from Kathy Coatney

CONTENTS

Dedication . . . . Pg iv

Acknowledgements . . . . Pg vi

From the Farm to the Table Olives. . . . . Pg 1

Vocabulary Word List . . . . Pg 28

Author Biography . . . . Pg 29

Dedication

To Farmer Charlie and Farmer Nick, with thanks for their time, expertise and entertaining stories. A special thanks to Lily for being the best model ever.

In Memoriam

In memory of Lily's daddy, Ryan. His goodness will shine down on us forever.

Acknowledgements

I've had a number of life-altering moments in my life, each special in their own way. The road to becoming a children's author has been smooth and rocky, but it has been an incredible journey because of those who have accompanied me.

My inspiration for the project, Georgia Bockoven; expert and consultant, Patti Thurman; email check-in pals, Jennifer Skullestad and Lisa Sorensen; and critique partner Luann Erickson, you are my GPS to finding the end. Friends and family who made the journey memorable: Karol Black, Tammy Lambeth, Libby Hall, Shari Boullion, Diana Robertson, Terry McLaughlin, and Patti Berg, you're the best. To my family, you for have been my inspiration. Thank you. I never would have made it without you.

I've also had the pleasure to work with several talented businesswomen: Susan Crosby, my editor; Yvonne Betancourt, my formatter, and Tara, my cover designer.

Note to parents and teachers: The underlined words are second-grade vocabulary words. A list of the words used can be found at the end of the book.

From the Farm to the Table Series

    From the Farm to the Table: Dairy
    From the Farm to the Table: Bees
    From the Farm to the Table: Olives

From the Farm to the Table: Olives

Farmer Charlie and Farmer Nick

Have you ever eaten olives off of your fingers? Farmer Charlie and Farmer Nick are olive guys, and they say that's the best way to eat olives. They know all kinds of things about olives. Like kids love olives. Like it's fun to eat olives off of your fingers. Like olives are good to eat and good for you.

Farmer Charlie and Farmer Nick love olives. They love them on their tacos, and sandwiches, and they <u>especially</u> like them on top of their pizza.

Manzanillo olives

Farmer Charlie and Farmer Nick raise table olives. Table olives are the kind of olives you eat from a can or jar. There are also olives that are made into olive oil.

Sevillano Olive

Farmer Charlie raises an olive variety called Sevillano (pronounced se/vee/yano). A variety is a specific type of olive. Sevillano olives come in different sizes. Medium, large, extra large, jumbo, colossal and super-colossal. Super-colossal is the <u>biggest</u> olive grown.

Farmer Charlie next to his Sevillano olive tree

Farmer Charlie's trees are really, really old. They were planted before 1900. That's over a century ago. A century is 100 years. A few olive trees are still alive that are over 3,000 years old. That's more than 30 centuries old. That's 30 times older than Farmer Charlie and Farmer Nick.

Farmer Charlie holding a Sevillano olive branch

Farmer Charlie loves farming, but he didn't become a farmer until after he was all grown up. One day a woman Farmer Charlie worked with brought in an olive branch from her Sevillano tree. It had <u>incredibly</u> big, green olives on it. Farmer Charlie thought it was the most <u>exquisite</u> tree he'd ever seen.

Farmer Charlie loved that his friend raised olives. In fact, he was so <u>impressed</u>, he bought a Sevillano orchard and became an olive farmer himself.

Farmer Nick checking his Manzanillo olives

Farmer Nick has always loved olive trees. He has worked in olive orchards since he was 13 years old. He earned extra money pruning, mowing, and irrigating the olive trees. It was hard work, but he didn't <u>complain</u> because he liked the work.

Farmer Nick raises table olives, too, but he raises a different variety of olive called Manzanillo (pronounced man/za/neeyo). He bought land and planted baby Manzanillo trees and started his own olive orchard.

Farmer Nick's farm is right next to Farmer Charlie's. They are neighbor farmers. They help each other out by sharing equipment. The <u>distance</u> between their farms is less than a mile. Did you know a mile is 5,280 feet?

Lily eating olives

Farmer Charlie's Sevillano trees grow giant olives that are big enough to fit on his fingers. Farmer Nick's olives are smaller, and they fit on kid-sized fingers. Both varieties are delicious to eat!

Manzanillo olives

Farmer Charlie has 20 rows of Sevillano trees, and there are 35 trees in each row. He has a total of 700 trees. Farmer Nick has 20 rows of Manzanillo trees, and there are 50 trees in each row. He has a total of 1,000 trees.

All year long Farmer Nick and Farmer Charlie take care of their olive trees. Springtime is a very busy time of year because that's when they have to prune or thin out the branches on their trees. To remove smaller branches they use pruning shears.

To remove larger branches they use chain saws and pole saws. After the trees are pruned, the limbs or brush that were cut from the trees are chopped or burned.

Farmer Nick showing Manzanillo olives in bloom

In May, the olive trees bloom, and there are thousands of tiny white blossoms all over the trees. After about a month, the blossoms are gone and tiny olives begin to develop. It takes from May through October, which is 6 months, before the olives are ready for harvest.

Sevillano Tree

Farmer Nick and Farmer Charlie monitor the olives closely, and if they <u>notice</u> the olives starting to shrivel or get wrinkled, they give them more water. The olives, and the trees, need plenty of water because water keeps them alive, just like it does for people.

Manzanillo olive orchard

Trees also need nitrogen, which is a fertilizer. Fertilizer is food for the trees and the olives. Farmer Charlie and Farmer Nick give them fertilizer at just the right time to make the olives grow big, and fat, and plump.

Lily holding unripe Manzanillo olives.

Table olives are different from other fruits like peaches or cherries that are picked when they are ripe. Table olives are picked green, unripe, and they ripen after they are picked. If you eat them straight from the tree they are bitter and taste icky.

Farmer Charlie pouring Manzanillo olives into a bin

Olives are measured by how many tons are picked from each acre of trees. A ton is 2,000 pounds. Farmer Charlie has 10 acres, and Farmer Nick has 6 acres. If Farmer Charlie harvested five tons per acre, he would have 50 tons of olives total. Farmer Nick would have 30 tons of olives total.

Box of Sevillano olives

In the fall, Farmer Nick and Farmer Charlie hire workers to pick the olives. Almost all of the table olives are picked by hand, but a few are harvested with a mechanical harvester. The workers climb ladders and pick the olives into a bucket. The olives are poured into a box that weighs 50 pounds when it is loaded.

Bin of Manzanillo olives

The boxes are poured into a bin. Each bin holds 1,000 pounds of olives. When the bin is full, it is driven to the processing plant.

Manzanillo olives

Olives are naturally green. The processing is what makes them black. The first step in processing olives is to put them into a lye curing solution to take out the bitterness. This takes several days.

Next, the olives go through a series of cold-water rinses to remove every bit of curing solution. During the curing process, air is bubbled through the olives. Air is what makes them black. At the very end of the processing, a tiny bit of organic iron salt is sometimes added to keep the olives dark black after they are canned.

Sevillano olives that were cured in salt brine

Another type of processing cures the olives in salt brine. The olives remain in the brine tank for at least four months.

    After the olives are processed, they are sorted and packed. Some olives are left whole with the pits inside, some have a machine remove the pit, and some are sliced or chopped. How do you <u>prefer</u> your olives? Farmer Charlie likes his in tacos.

Farmer Charlie and Farmer Nick say raising olives is a very important job. They like knowing that all the care and work they put into their olive trees makes finger-licking good food for kids to eat.

The End

Vocabulary Word List

Biggest
Complain
Distance
Especially
Exquisite
Impressed
Incredibly
Notice
Prefer

Author Biography

Kathy Coatney has spent long hours behind the lens of a camera wading through rice paddies, dairies and orchards during her twenty-five year career as a photojournalist specializing in agriculture. She and her husband grow table olives and her family roots in agriculture run four generations deep, so Kathy knows farming from the ground up. Concerned that kids today don't have the exposure to farms and rural life that teaches them how their food is produced, she envisioned a new direction for her writing and launched From the Farm to the Table, a series of nonfiction children's books about agriculture. Kathy also loves — and writes — deeply emotional, small-town contemporary romances.

Visit her website at: www.kathycoatney.com

www.ingramcontent.com/pod-product-compliance
Lightning Source LLC
Chambersburg PA
CBHW050757110526
44588CB00002B/36